Turning Back the Pa Maid Marian Wa

Preface

Turning Back the Pages is a series that aims to bring the past back to life through bygone photographs and other images. This volume, on Nottingham's Maid Marian Way, brings the series into a period of 'living memory' and includes key contemporary images that can be used to help compare old and new landscapes. It has been compiled by Chris Weir, Senior Archivist (Public Services) and Nick Smith, Archives Assistant, largely from photographs and other documents held by Nottinghamshire Archives. Most of the historic photographs were selected from the Nottingham City Design and Property Services collection (CA/DP) and the Nottingham and District Co-operative collection (DD/GN). This publication will appeal to anyone who remembers the building of Maid Marian Way or who has an interest in the development of modern urban landscapes.

Mark Dorrington, Team Manager Archives and Local Studies

Looking North Towards Friar Lane, May 1964. The route of Maid Marian Way bulldozed through a series of historic streets including Castle Gate and Hounds Gate. The new entrance to Hounds Gate is visible on the left of the photograph.

Front Cover:

New Horizons. This dramatic aerial view of Maid Marian May was taken in August 1966. It shows the road nearing completion. Multi-storey offices loom over the new road as this part of old Nottingham began to disappear under concrete and tarmac.

Introduction

'Turning Back The Pages of Maid Marian Way' provides a unique insight into the building and development of Nottingham's most controversial street. You either love it or you hate it! For some it's a bold and exciting example of modern construction and an innovative solution to urban traffic flow. To others it represents all that is bad in modern urban planning and design. A whole chunk of Nottingham's historic landscape was sacrificed to the car. With this book you can make up your own mind. As you 'turn back the pages' you are taken on a walk from the south end of Maid Marian Way (Broad Marsh/Canal Street) to the north end (Derby Road/Chapel Bar). There are photographs of pre-demolition streets and properties, the new road and buildings under construction; and there are present-day images so that all along the 'trail' you can re-create the contemporary landscape.

Maid Marian Way was a no-nonsense creation of Nottingham's post-war era. Its 1960s concrete blocks and its sheer scale have all provoked strong reactions in the hearts and minds of Nottingham's people and visitors to Nottingham. As the dramatic gash in the landscape forced its way through a series of the City's most historic streets, Arthur Ling, Professor of Town Planning at Nottingham University, declared the street, in 1965, to be an 'insult to Maid Marion' (sic) and added that it 'must qualify as one of the ugliest in Europe'.

Yet Maid Marian Way was not a product of the Sixties, its origins were in post-war redevelopment planning. As early as 1943 a key report by the City's Reconstruction Committee identified the need to tackle the problem of traffic congestion and proposed, as part of a series of measures, a new inner ring road to link Canal Street and Parliament Street. The road, later to become Maid Marian Way, was to follow the line of Walnut Tree Lane, Granby Street and the lower end of Park Row. The aim was to 'carry a considerable amount of traffic that requires to approach the centre of the City without actually entering it'. As the years went by various schemes in the report were shelved, including a new civic centre, as traffic congestion worsened, the need for road schemes became more urgent. Work on the new inner ring road began in the late 1950s. In 1958 a meeting of the General Works & Highways Committee resolved that the new road be called Maid Marian Way. That same year saw the demolition of Collin's Almshouses, built in 1709, on Friar Lane, to make way for the new development.

Construction of Maid Marian Way was slow and complicated. It involved substantial demolition, road widening, new road foundations and surfacing, the building of a pedestrian island, high-rise office blocks and other buildings alongside the new road. By the mid-Sixties the new road neared completion. It was clear that the car was now 'king' and the new 'Way' sat in a canyon of looming concrete blocks. The Sixties had arrived in Nottingham. As the years went by it became evident that Nottingham residents resented the loss of historic properties for Maid Marian Way. Both residents and visitors faced a grim prospect in negotiating a route from the City centre up to Nottingham Castle and the Park area. Then, in the last decade of the 20th century, a series of major improvements to the Way and its surroundings, were begun as part of what was known as 'The Turning Point'.

Paving was renewed, bushes and trees were planted in the middle of the carriageway, and the sunken pedestrian 'plaza' was demolished and replaced by a modern crossing. If you walk along Maid Marian Way today this book will take you right back through its controversial history and the photographs will evoke many memories of the past.

Collins Hospital (Almshouses), Friar Lane, 19 August 1958. Although the photograph suggests a tranquil summer's day at the almshouses, the reality was very different. Demolition of the building was already underway as part of the Maid Marian Way development.

Canal Street, August 1962. Traffic at the junction of Canal Street and Grey Friar Gate and what was to become the southern end of Maid Marian Way.

Grey Friar Gate, 1960. The buildings in the foreground included the Astoria Garage and the Denman Hotel. These buildings were eventually demolished to make way for the Broad Marsh development.

Grey Friar Gate and the Sherwood Rooms, April 1964. The Sherwood Rooms was originally known as the Astoria Ballroom. It is now the Ocean Night Club.

Advertising Brochure for the Sherwood Rooms, 1964. It has always been one of Nottingham's leading venues for concerts and dancing.
Nottinghamshire Archives DD 2450/3/6/3

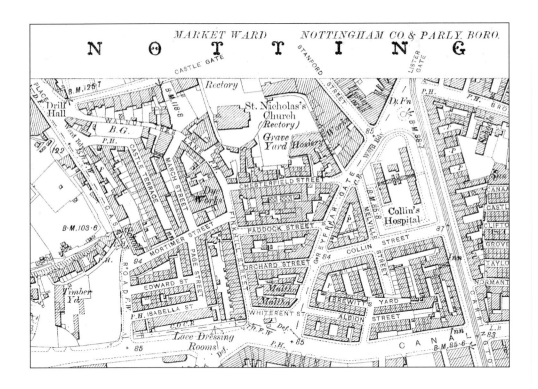

Ordnance Survey Map of 1901. The streets shown disappeared in the late 1950s and Sixties. Walnut Tree Lane extended from the junction of Castle Gate and Castle Road southwards into Finkhill Street.

Jessamine Cottages, Castle Road. The cottages were demolished in 1956 to make way for People's College. This view of the Cottages was drawn by local artist Marjorie Bates (1886-1962). *Nottinghamshire Archives XPR 9/12*

JESSAMINE COTTAGES, NOTTINGHAM.

Walnut Tree Lane.
This 1965 edition of the 'Nottinghamshire Countryside' shows an earlier view of Walnut Tree Lane.

End of an Era, October 1963. The last remnants of properties off Walnut Tree Lane. Just visible on the right is the Salutation Inn on Maid Marian Way.

Building Site, People's College, March 1957. This view looks towards Nottingham Castle and The Trip to Jerusalem.

Castle College, 2009. Looking northwards from the bottom of Maid Marian Way.

People's College Under Construction in 1958. The original People's College, on College Street on the edge of the Park, was opened in 1847. The new building was completed in 1959 and officially opened on the 23 March 1961.

Castle College, 2009 (formerly People's College).

In the Shadow of Broad Marsh. A view northwards from under the elevated concrete roadway in June 1969.

Eastwards Across Castle Road. Construction of People's College is underway in 1958.

St Nicholas' Church Trust School Under Demolition in 1949. The school opened on Castle Road in 1859. Surviving log books for the school date from 1863 to 1904. The school stood empty for many years prior to demolition.

Bottle Store for Laing & Co, February 1949.

Just in view behind Laings was the Colonel Hutchinson public house - the advert would have been for Tennant's Rock Ales. Colonel Hutchinson held Nottingham Castle for the Parliamentarians during the Civil War. The building stood on the corner of Castle Road and Castle Terrace.

St Nicholas' Rectory, Castle Gate, May 1957. The Rectory was demolished during 1957. The building stood directly in line with Maid Marian Way. In the forefront is a sign for the Royal Children public house.

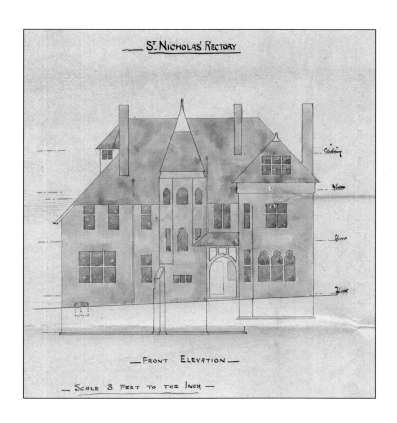

Elevation for St Nicholas' Rectory, 1886. The architect of the Rectory was Watson Fothergill. He was one of the City's leading architects.
Nottinghamshire Archives CA/PL 23/46

Planning Control Application for St Nicholas' Rectory, March 1886. Under building control legislation introduced in the 1870s plans for new buildings had to be submitted to local authorities for approval.
Nottinghamshire Archives CA/PL 23/46

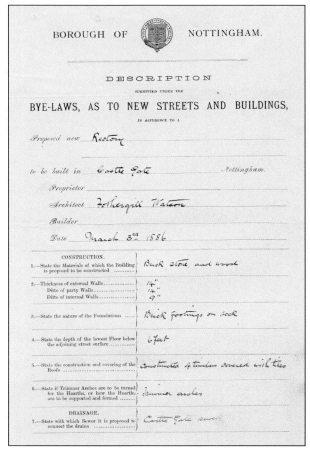

THE ST. NICHOLAS ANNUITY FUND.

(Founded by the late MISS SARAH PETTIFOR.)

RULES.

1.—The Charity shall be called or designated "The Saint Nicholas Annuity Fund."

2.—The Persons eligible as Pensioners shall be needy Ladies, Spinsters or Widows resident in the City of Nottingham, or the immediate neighbourhood.

3—No Person shall be eligible who is under Fifty Years of Age, or is in receipt of Parochial Relief, or is of Unsound Mind.

4—In order to be eligible, a Candidate must be of good Moral Character, and shall reside in England, and all things being equal, preference shall be given to residents within the City and County of Nottingham.

5—No Person shall be eligible as a Pensioner who has a Private Income of more than Forty Pounds per annum.

6—Rule 5 may from time to time be varied by the Charity Trustees for the time being, in case any such changes should take place in the relative value of money and of the necessaries of life, as in their judgment to render a variation of the rule desirable.

7—Every Candidate for a Pension shall make her application in writing under her hand, containing a declaration according to a form approved by the Charity Trustees as to the several matters hereinbefore mentioned in Rules 2, 3, 4, and 5, and shall furnish a testimonial by two well-known and respectable persons, and such Candidate or Applicant shall also furnish a Certificate or other satisfactory proof of her age.

8—The Documents furnished as mentioned in the last preceding Rule shall be filed, and upon each such application there shall be made in a book to be kept for the purpose, and called "The Application Book," an entry specifying the date of the application, and the Name, Age, Residence, and qualification of the Applicant.

9—There shall also be kept in a book to be provided for that purpose, and to be called "The Pensioners' Book," a register wherein shall be entered the names of the persons elected as Pensioners, and the dates of their respective elections, and the date and mode of the occurrence of any vacancy.

10—Pensioners shall be elected by the Charity Trustees at a meeting held according to the Regulations hereinafter contained with respect to meetings of the Charity Trustees.

11—Every Pensioner on her election shall sign a Memorandum in such form as the Charity Trustees shall from time to time approve, undertaking to give immediate notice to such Trustees, in case she should marry, or in case her private income should at any time amount to or exceed the yearly sum of Forty Pounds, exclusive of the Pension.

12—Each Pension shall be the yearly sum of Twenty Pounds, and shall be payable Half-Yearly, and each Half-Yearly instalment shall be paid at the end of the current Half-Year.

13—If any Pensioner marries or becomes entitled to an additional income, so as to make up her private income independently of her Pension to more than Forty Pounds, her Pension shall thereupon cease.

14—The Charity Trustees shall have the power to suspend or take away the Pension of any Pensioner in case of any deficiency in the Income of the Charity, or in case of the Pensioner being guilty of immorality, or ceasing to satisfy the Conditions of Rule 4, or for any other reason which in the opinion of such Trustees may render such a step necessary, or desirable. Any withdrawal, whether permanent or temporary, of a Pension under this Rule, shall be determined upon at a Special Meeting, or at any Ordinary Meeting, in the Circular convening which, Notice shall have been given of the intention to propose such withdrawal.

15—Subject to the preceding Rules, Pensioners shall be entitled to their Pensions for their Lives.

St Nicholas' Annuity Fund for Needy Ladies c 1920. Under the Fund each female pensioner over 50 years old received a yearly sum of £20.
Nottinghamshire Archives PR 19142/1

Looking South Towards Canal Street, August 1958. Construction work in the foreground shows the area where St Nicholas' Rectory once stood until its demolition.

St Nicholas' Church, 2009.
An earlier church was taken down during the Civil War but a new church was built in the 1670s. It was re-consecrated in 1678.

View of Maid Marian Way Showing St Nicholas' Church, September 1961.
The use of the frontage area for cars, scooters and motorbikes illustrates contemporary problems with traffic and parking.

Castle Gate, 2009. This part of Castle Gate was saved from demolition and some of the buildings were adapted for a Costume Museum for the City (now closed).

Castle Gate No's 53-55 in 1949. Looking towards St Nicholas' Rectory which is just visible on the left of the photograph. The street, entirely cobbled, was one of the most historic in Nottingham.

Castle Gate (North Side), 1949. Looking eastwards towards the Royal Children public house. The properties in the foreground were demolished.

The Royal Children, January 1958. The Royal Children was largely rebuilt in the 1930s. An old whalebone once stood over the door entrance but was moved to an inside parlour in more recent years.

The Salutation in 1956. This view of the Salutation is at the junction of Hounds Gate and St. Nicholas' Street. Though parts of the building date back to the 16th century, major rebuilding work was undertaken at the time of the Maid Marian Way development.

<table>
<tr><td colspan="2">City of Nottingham.</td><td>6997</td></tr>
</table>

WAR DAMAGE.

FIRST AID REPAIRS.

ADDRESS Ye Old Salutation Inn, St. Nicholas Street. 'Phone No.

OCCUPIER Percy R. Dridge. Description of Property Public house

OWNER Name Rateable Value
or AGENT : Address District Ref. Number G.10.

Damage caused by Air attack. Inspected by T. W. Javan. Date 9/5/41.

Report on Damage Ref. No. 7420. Category D.

Roof Slight. Walls -

Floors - Contents -

Generally Windows.

Repairs done by Address

Instructions given by Order No. Date

Bomb Damage Report on the Salutation Inn, May 1941. The report followed the heaviest bombing raid of the war on Nottingham during the night of the 8-9th May 1941. *Nottinghamshire Archives CA/AP 2/5/448/1*

The Salutation in 2009. Today the Salutation finds itself adjacent to Maid Marian Way and is dwarfed by a very large office block.

A New Skyline in the Making, January 1965. Construction of another new office block, by Newdigate House, begins to tower over Maid Marian Way.

Newdigate House, Castle Gate, 1962. Newdigate House was built around 1675. French General Marshall Tallard, who had been defeated by the Duke of Marlborough at Blenheim in 1704, was held at the House for many years.

Marshall Tallard's Garden in the Early 1700s. Tallard was an enthusiastic gardener and is thought to have introduced celery to Nottingham. *Nottinghamshire Archives XPR 9/14*

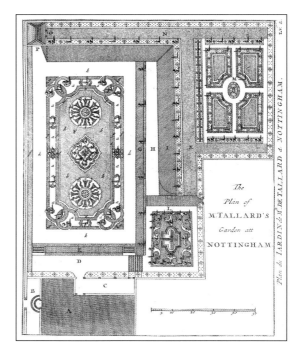

Looking Towards Collins' Almshouses, Friar Lane, August 1958. The almshouses were built in 1709. They were demolished at an early stage of the Maid Marian Way work during 1958. The architectural historian Nikolaus Pevsner described them as 'one of the best almshouses of its date in England'. In the event only a small part of the land on which the almshouses stood was used for the development.

Road Closed, October 1958. By this time the Collins' Almshouses had been demolished to make way for the new road.

Corner of Friar Lane, March 1963. On the corner there was a Municipal Car Park created temporarily from land that had been cleared. The modern block is Walton House.
Nottinghamshire Archives DD 1618/5

Looking Down Maid Marian Way From Walton House, October 1963. The older properties in the centre of the photograph were awaiting demolition.

Construction of Friar Lane Underpass, 1965. The underpass was also known as a 'sunken roundabout' or 'plaza'. It gave pedestrian access beneath Maid Marian Way.

Underpass Under Construction, August 1965. To allow space for the underpass the modern buildings were set back along new building lines.

Completed Underpass in May 1967. Pedestrian tunnels intersected a series of sloping concrete walls. The underpass aimed to link the City centre with the area around the Castle.

Preston & Son Kiosk, May 1967. This newsagents was a familiar landmark for over 30 years. It disappeared from the landscape when a 'surface' crossing with traffic lights replaced the underpass.

Entrance to Underpass, June 1966. Access through the underpass led under Maid Marian Way, linking the two sides of Friar Lane. City House is in the background.

Friar Lane Junction, March 1965. New buildings rapidly appear on the horizon, including City House, on the left, which included the Maid Marian Café on the ground floor.

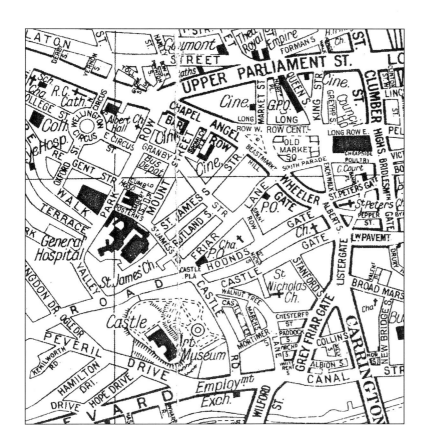

Geographia Map c 1957. The map shows the street layout of the area between Canal Street and Chapel Bar before redevelopment for Maid Marian Way.

Looking North From the Friar Lane Junction, May 1965. The top end of Maid Marian Way was created from Granby Street.

Maid Marian Way, 2009.
The view is at the corner of Maid Marian Way and Friar Lane. The Sixties landscape was a combination of offices, a multi-storey car park and the Brittania Hotel (formerly The Albany).

Looking South From the Junction of Granby Street and Mount Street, November 1962. Walton House and the rear of the Odeon Cinema are seen on the left behind the Barton Transport Bus Station. By 1965 the offices and original Hearty Good Fellow pub on the right would be demolished to make way for a multi-storey hotel and shopping complex.

Granby Street, 1963. Within two years Granby Street would disappear and become part of the new, inner city, ring road. Walton House stands on the right.

St James' Street, 5 November 1963. This view is at the junction of Granby Street with St James' Street. St James' Street still had its traditional cobbled surface.

Luxury Coach Tours
Through England—Scotland and Wales
—inclusive fares
—first-class Hotel Accommodation

Express Seaside Services
Blackpool—Skegness—Scarborough
Cleethorpes—Mablethorpe and
Great Yarmouth

Seasonal Excursions
To local beauty spots—sporting events
and places of interest

TRENT
MOTOR TRACTION Co LTD

Booking Offices: HUNTINGDON STREET OMNIBUS STATION   Telephone: 45601 (6 lines)
And MOUNT STREET OMNIBUS STATION

Advert for Trent Bus Excursions and Coach Tours, 1956 – 1957. Trent Motor Traction Company ran a variety of trips from Mount Street and Huntingdon Street bus stations. The advert was published in the Nottingham Official Handbook. The model shown is a Leyland Tiger Cub.

Mount Street Bus Station, Early 1960s.
In the post-war years Mount Street was one of the principal bus stations in the City, providing a terminus for Trent, Barton & Midland General.
Picture the Past (website)
NT GM 008581

MOUNT STREET.
(Angel row.) Mk.

5 Richards' Boot Repairers Limited
9 Scott Mrs. Vera, herbalist
11 Wright Thomas, hair dresser
Barker Hy. Ltd. cabinet makers &c
19 Belshaw Robert, antique dealer
.... Pleasant place ....
21 Smith Thomas, hardware dealer
25 Clower Edwin Thomas, currier
27 Soar William, shopkeeper
.... Bromley place ....
31 Smart Mrs. Clara, glass &c. dlr
.... Exchange court ....
37 Hawksley Sidney, baker
Mount court—
...27 Farmer William, boot maker
...28 Attenborough Miss Mary Ann,
     news agent
39 Fitzer Mrs. Sarah Ann, shopkeepr
43 Gavin Peter, v.Hearty Good Fellow
.... Mount square ....
Goater Charles & Son, printers &c
51 Willsons, printers & stationers
65 Hancock & Son, blouse manufactrs
67 & 69 Cantie Switch Co. Limited
69 Hall George, wicker chair maker
73 Poyzer Roland, tailor
.... Wilson's yard ....
... St. James' ter. & Postern street ...
                 (Cross over
... Kendall st. & Cumberland place ...
50 Webb John Hickling, shopkeeper
48 Willis Mrs. Rose
46 Padey Mrs. Eliza
40 Bailey E. & Co. waste paper dlrs
40 Goulding Wm. & Arth. plumbers
40 Mullineux Henry Ernest, joiner
40 Hudson & Russell, basket makers
Jacques Bros. Ltd. clothing manufrs
34 Brealey & Jessop, engineers
32 Smith Frederick William, v. Sir
   Francis Burdett
28 Curtis Charles, shopkeeper
26 Hooton Mrs. Betsy, shopkeeper
.... Crammer's place ....
24 Duffy John, egg dealer
.... Budge row ....
22 Hollis William, boot maker
.... Pembridge place ....
St. Thomas' Mission Hall
.... Mount Pleasant ....
16 Gale A. G. who. sweet merchant
14 Marshall Abraham, ticket writer
12 Cumberland Mrs. Eliza, greengro
.... Olive row ....
.... Every place ....
6 & 8 Webb C. W. & Co. cardboard
   box makers
...Gordon A. & Co. paper merchants
...Phillips Jn. Chas.rope & twine mer
4 Barnett Wm. Jas. v. Britannia
2 Flint George, greengrocer
2 Searson George, printer
.... Chapel bar ....

Wright's Directory, Mount Street,

1920. A wide variety of trades is listed in the entry, including a rope and twine merchant, basket maker, wicker chair maker, printer, baker, hairdresser and herbalist.

Oral History Transcript

This edited extract was from an interview with 'Peggy' who lived in a small square just off Mount Street. It was recorded in 1983.
(Courtesy of Nottingham City Council, Leisure & Community Services, Nottingham Central Library).

Whereabouts were you born? **Mount Street you know, where the bus station is, that's where I was born, number 11, Mount Square, Mount Street in 1922…I 'ad to set the fire for me Mum, 'cos she 'ad to go to work at 5am in the morning; she was cleaning in the Lace Market…. she could make something out of nothing me Mum could. We ate bread and butter pudding, jam roly-poly pudding, rice pudding, sago and tapioca…we never 'ad chips, it was boiled potatoes, stews & things. The worst times was in the winter – many a time we sat in the dark 'cos Mum hadn't a penny to put in the gas'.**

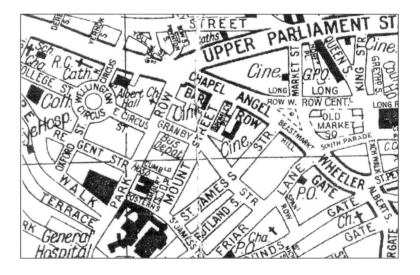

A Section of Geographia Map, 1957. The section highlights the area from Chapel Bar to Friar Lane that was cut in two by Maid Marian Way. Mount Street Bus Station is labelled as 'Bus Depot'.

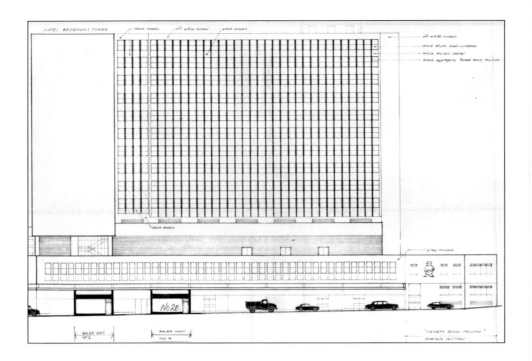

Plans for New Shops (Former Granby Street). The plan (September 1970) includes a new hotel behind the shops and, on the corner with Mount Street, the Hearty Good Fellow Public House. A pub had stood on the site since around 1800. *Nottinghamshire Archives CA/PL 2/145/9/70*

Aerial View From Walton House Towards Park Row, 1963. The old ABC Cinema roof is in the foreground and just visible is Co-operative House. Large areas of Park Row, the Albert Hotel and many other buildings were soon to be demolished.

No's 2-10 Park Row, April 1964. The entire section of the Row was to disappear to make way for the new road developments. The County Coroner's office was on Park Row for many years.

Nottingham's Ancient Town Wall, October 1967. In the course of Park Row's demolition the borough's ancient town wall was revealed for a short time.

No's 7-15 Park Row, September 1963. This view of Park Row, opposite no's 2-10, leads into the junction with Parliament Street. The three-storey building is the Church of England Building Society. The adjacent building with the central triangular pediment was a painter and decorators (Sparrow & Son) that had existed from Victorian times. Co-operative House is just visible on Parliament Street.

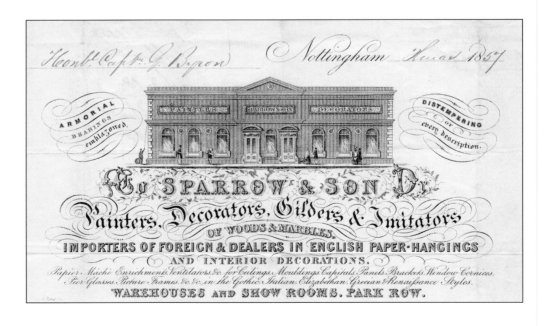

Letterhead of Sparrow & Son, 1857. Sparrow & Son was a 'Painters, Decorators, Gilders and Imitators'.
Nottinghamshire Archives M 7560/48

Chapel Bar, From Charles Deering's 'History of Nottingham' 1751. This last surviving mediaeval gateway into the town was demolished in 1743.

Ordnance Survey Map, 1901. The path of Maid Marian Way was to cut through the middle of many of the streets in the area, emerging at Chapel Bar.

Co-op Shop on the North Side of the Chapel Bar Island c. 1963. The Albert Hotel can just be seen behind the Co-op.

The North Side of Chapel Bar, 1973. A Co-op Garage and store faced the traffic island. The store included a butchery, optical, floral and greengrocery departments.

The Co-op Shop and Garage, Chapel Bar, 1973. These buildings were demolished during 1973. The site is now occupied by the City Gate Offices, the Gate House pub and Toll House Hill, the road that leads down from Clarendon Street to Chapel Bar.

Chapel Bar in 2009. This photograph looks westwards up Derby Road. St Barnabas' Cathedral spire, on the left, highlights the only building to survive from an earlier era in this view. On the right are City Gate Offices East and West.

Acknowledgements

All the historic photographs and documents are published courtesy of Nottinghamshire Archives, except the photograph of Mount Street Bus Station (Reference: NT GM 008581) that is reproduced by permission of Nottingham City Library & Information Service: Department of Sport, Culture and Parks (via Picture The Past). The modern (2009) photographs are reproduced by permission of the photographer Chris Weir.

View Towards Friar Lane Junction, 1965. The building on the right is the Green Shield Trading Stamp Company 'Gift House'.

For thousands more images of Nottingham and Nottinghamshire visit www.picturethepast.org.uk

© 2011 Nottinghamshire County Council

ISBN 9780-902751-712